SLIPPERY CHARACTERS

This book is for Margli

who keeps my words honest

SLIPPERY
CHARACTERS

Poems & Poetics

Paul Matthews

Paul Matthews.

FIVE SEASONS PRESS 2011

Published by
Five Seasons Press
41 Green Street
Hereford HR1 2QH

ISBN 978-0-947960-64-3

The emblems and letterings were made by Katharina Kubin, taking inspiration from *The Lindisfarne Gospels* and various other artefacts and trinkets. The photograph of a lugworm cast on the cover was taken by Christine Meyer on that other holy island of Iona. The design on page 85 draws upon another of her photographs.

Acknowledgements

Some of these pieces have appeared in the following publications:

Resurgence; Caduceus; New View; Scintilla; Tears in the Fence; The Golden Blade; Walking the Dog; Soundings; The Ariadne Newsletter; Into the Further Reaches (PS Avalon); *The Fabulous Names of Things* (privately printed*); The Empty Hill* (Skylark Press); *Words in Place* (Hawthorn Press).

The versions published here supersede all previous ones.

Typeset in 13 on 16pt Arno
at Five Seasons Press
and printed on Five Seasons recycled paper
by the MPG Book Group, Bodmin & King's Lynn

CONTENTS

Word on Word

Um

Um is a good word
to begin a sermon with

though my friend says
there isn't a place for it
within the flow of speech.

Erm . . . A U M . . . I'm
humming my way back
into that quiet syllable.

It murmurs behind stars.
All babies mumble it.

Please, friend, permit
this tingle on my lips
before I speak. Amen.
My sermon's ended.

No Words Yet

It is ten o'clock on a Monday morning, and as I hesitate with my pen in the air I feel the stream of what I mean to write gathering in the muscles of my arm, and I can trace it further to a tension around my heart that has no words yet.

All the spellbound sounds that formed me before ever I could trace an alphabet are flooding back to me this morning: the clink of milk bottles; blackbird on the silver birch; Jack Spratt; Little Jack Horner; Jack-I'm-Off-To-Seek-My-Fortune jiggety jolt upon the old carthorse that was my mother's knee; leaf murmur; ruffle of pages; The Fierth Bad Wabbit; Jason and the Golden Fleas; The Lion the Witch and the time when far too advanced for me but my ear was open my mother spoke Milton's words by heart of Satan tumbling headlong into Hell because at that time and a long time after she felt perdition was her own condition. Or in London with my father back from the war we would go down to the river looking for Saxon harps in the mud when the tide was out. He read me the story of the Great Fire which destroyed the old St Paul's Cathedral in the very place of its burning, yes, and what about all those Bible stories that got stocked up in my bones when I was a choirboy in Exeter so that now as I write I expect everyone to know them? And as my pen gathers momentum I find myself within the resonances of a shell, not knowing among the sea sounds that surround me whether I speak or listen or how to hold the thread of what I am trying to say when all these inflections and innuendoes and embedded metaphors from childhood and half-forgotten books and back to Babylon keep meaning themselves through me.

The Aleph

What better place to start than with the letter A. *The beginning of learning and the door of heaven*, is what that madman Christopher Smart called it. Its shape comes from the head of an Ox, they say, and 'Ox', according to my dictionary, is,

1: *Any bovine animal.* 2: *Castrated male of the domestic species.* It was Smart's strong conviction that there is life in language, a generative power. The current view of the matter, however, would go along with the gelded version, holding that language is a domestic arrangement, an information technology which in itself is devoid of life and mystery. I suppose that ever since people began to think about language, instead of simply living inside the spell of it, a tension has existed between these two views—the magical and the rational. Perhaps the very act of thinking about words is what severs the Ox from its magic potency. That; or in encountering some untamed element of the Aleph we do indeed stand in jeopardy of being tossed into a madness.

Weak-minded people, wrote Arthur Rimbaud, *beginning by thinking about the first letter of the alphabet, would soon rush into madness.* In the overweening confidence of his youth when, by his own confession, he considered himself *Magus or Angel, exempt from all morality*, he made that famous sonnet in which he claims that each vowel has a colour, and that the sounding of them conjures up images in the mind: *A, black velvety jacket of brilliant flies which buzz around cruel smells, gulfs of shadow.* Following a deliberate path of poetic initiation, he battered at the conventions imposed on language by the *one-eyed intellect* until its vowels became for him five Halleluiahs heralding a change of consciousness. *One must be deader than a fossil*, he wrote, *to finish a dictionary in any language.* And yet only a couple of years later, at the point of renouncing poetry altogether, he dismissed his 'Alchemy of the Word' with its rules for *the form and movement of each consonant* as one of his *follies*. I can understand why he did so. He was, for sure, rushing into madness through his *rational disordering of all the senses*. But I am not prepared to admit that he merely *invented* this overlap between words and movement, sound and image. Was it folly when he wrote, *The first adventure on the path was when a flower told me its name*? I don't believe so, even though, in leaving his tormented adolescence behind, he felt the need to spurn such magic. I, too, seek such a communion through language, and this is served by attending to the cadence of each line and sentence and to the colour of every sound in context until language becomes a substance shared as well as a communication about a subject.

How could I dismiss it when, in the depth of their craft, some of the poets I most admire admit to a sense that the sap of language streams within the veins of nature and sustains her? Robert Duncan, for instance: *As I came needing wonder as the new shoots need water / to the letter A that sounds its mystery in Wave and in Wane / trembling I bent as if there were a weight in words*. Or, going further back, there is Samuel Taylor Coleridge with his dream vision of Kubla Khan's garden *where Alph the sacred river ran / Through caverns measureless to man*—the images, he claimed, rising up before him *as things, with a parallel production of their correspondent expressions*.

Or I think of William Blake's description of the innocent poet who, plucking a reed to use as a *rural pen*, dips it in the stream for ink, as if to allow Nature herself to trace her alphabet. The further back we go, in fact, the more we find that the very sounds and rhythms of the language give voice to the elemental qualities of the local landscape. No doubt Dr Johnson, in the eighteenth century, felt justified in his attempt to have the meanings and spellings *reduced to alphabets* within the confines of his famous dictionary, for how, with a *wild and barbarous jargon* that refused to lie down in its stall, could the scientists of his time record the results of their experiments? I, too, love lexicons; yet how savourless my measured words seem compared to the Hey Diddle Diddles and Hopscotch rhymes of childhood, or the rocks and cliffs that utter themselves through the consonants of those Scops and Gleemen who first forged our language.

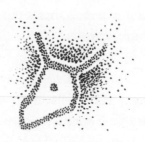

Axe and Pen
(The mumblings of Humbaba)

Every time you pick up your pen
it twists into a blade that makes me tremble.

The groves fold beneath it, glades
where I would lie in the sun
as the deer approached unafraid
and licked my cheekbones.

I was the guardian there, each twig
my fingertip. My mind was in it, stretched
ten thousand leagues the seven ways.

I remember the day you swung my gate open
crying *I will stamp my name in this place
lest oblivion take me.*

Ah, but it was my place, my Country
of the Living. I had a woman's eyes,
ten thousand this way that way, and you
shied yours away because I lacked alphabets.

I sent you visions, beautiful and wild;
but when you stepped close to the heart
of my abode you couldn't keep your eyelids open

for you are a man mindful of your name,
and in my place an epithet soon loses itself
among the many syllables the leaves are busy with.

Humbaba is my name, murmur of winds, hubbub
of baby talk. All the time you are writing

I am the shadow at your shoulder saying
axe and pen, they share a handle.

I had seven splendours once.

They are lumbered now in the cold
catalogue of things; and as you sigh for fame
you seldom hear the rustlings of my country.

Walking the Dog

Confident in what we mean to say, we choose words carefully; but even as we do so some ancient pedigree, refusing to lie down in its dictionary, tugs at the leash, sniffing among the roots a syllable intent upon its own mythologies.

Long buried bones this dog digs up. We are dogged by metaphors and doctrines that howl to us from the strata'd mouths of ten millennia back—fearful images marrowed in seemingly dry abstractions.

And, digging down through the last lettery detritus, it's Cerberus himself we find—three-headed hound of Hades—who must be appeased with a crust if ever our words are to mean what we mean them to mean.

Throw him a word, and he'll crack it open with his teeth and spew etymologies out which threaten to bewilder us with multiple meanings when only one was intended.

I'm a little afraid of this three-tongued mongrel straining there beneath the crust of language and, at the same time, I am excited to be both walked and walking on this path of unpredictable arrival.

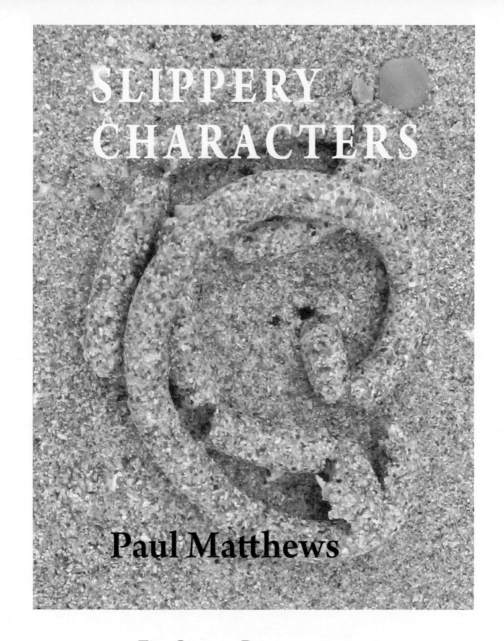

SLIPPERY CHARACTERS

Paul Matthews

Five Seasons Press announces
the March 2011 publication
of Paul Matthews' new collection of
poems and poetics

SLIPPERY CHARACTERS
Poems & Poetics
Paul Matthews

In this first gathering of his poetry since *The Ground that Love Seeks* (1996) Paul Matthews explores aspects of biography 'at the verge of the mythological'. Writing of his strong experiences in the mountains of California, at Ephesus, on the holy island of Lindisfarne, he is keenly aware that the words and alphabets under his pen come charged with the fibs and fables of millennia back, a more than personal will which must be wrestled with, surrendered to at times, as he shapes his present purposes.

The dynamic relationship between word and world is central to this book, the 'slippery characters' of its title being both the mythological, historical, human and animal beings that inhabit these pages and the written characters themselves whose images and gestures spring to life through the emblems and letterings created by Katharina Kubin.

ISBN 978-0-947960-64-3

Thoughtfully designed and generously proportioned
(Metric Royal 8vo / 234×156mm / over 9 × 6")
88 pages printed offset-litho
on high quality acid-free Five Seasons recycled paper
section-sewn with flapped limp jacket

Available in the UK from

Five Seasons Press, 41 Green Street, Hereford HR1 2QH
books@fiveseasonspress.com
at £12.50 plus £3.00 post & packing

And in the United States from

Celia Riahi, 135 Cottage St., Amherst, MA 01002
celiariahi@gmail.com
at $25 plus $6 shipping for one copy (plus $1 for each additional copy)
Other US shipping options (and rates for Canada) may be requested from Celia Riahi

Word and World

I am looking at a page that Eadfrith made thirteen centuries ago on the island of Lindisfarne. It is the opening of St John's Gospel—*In Principio erat verbum*—except that in the way he wrote it all the letters run into each other, making the reading difficult. *Inthebeginningwastheword.* He made it in honour of his friend, St Cuthbert.

When I was a child I often stayed with relations just across from 'Holy Island', as we called it. At low tide, when we drove over the causeway, my grandmother, who had a high regard for words, would warn us not to say *pig* lest we shocked the natives. Why? Maybe St Cuthbert himself decreed it when he was Bishop on Lindisfarne.

There are no such *articles* (as pigs had to be called) in the book that Eadfrith gave us. But I do see that the letters are woven about with all kinds of other animals: dogs' heads, sea snakes, a bird nestled into God's own Name, long green cormorants insinuating their necks into every cranny of divinity.

Bewilderment is my first response; these Celtic knots and DNAs embroidering this Saxon page whirl me away, make me giddy. Clearly, in the beginning, God's creatures are not yet settled inside their skins! But, if I dare to keep looking, I note that the patterns do eventually resolve themselves, holding some order within this chaos. Why does he turn the 'N' of the first word on its side? I reckon it's to say that clarity of communication is not his only purpose.

In the beginning was the Word. St John was his favourite saint, I think. This is my favourite page. How beautifully he accommodates the creatures of the island within the 'In' with which St John begins his gospel!

Every morning (so my grandmother told me) St Cuthbert stood up to his neck in the icy water. The seals came to lick him warm and dry. One onion and one leek a week, that's how he feasted.

But this wonderful book that Eadfrith made for him shows little sign of such mortification. It is true that, to humble himself before his Maker, he leaves corners of the work unfinished. But look how Creation is held there within the Word and the Word is resonant in every vein and spiral of Creation. That is what I long for—this seemingly impossible thing—to speak a language which is not hitched on to nature, not just words about the world, but one with it.

Skill alone does not achieve this. I do not envy Eadfrith his cold hands. I am glad that the North Sea storms can't reach me in my scriptorium. Yet it is only through such a courageous dedication to his craft, sustained by his great love for the Logos revealed in the least of creatures, that he achieves this union of word and image, allowing the rhythms of the waves, the cries of the kittiwakes, to wash over the margins of his page and into the blues and greens that he is shaping.

Years later, when he was in his grave and his island desecrated, his book got lost in the sea. Then somebody dreamt to look for it on the beach when the tide was out and there it was, miraculously preserved for us. With so much sea associated with the thing no wonder its characters keep shifting away from my attempts to read them.

It was a fine inspiration to portray *Johannis aquila* as the one Gospel writer without a pen in his fist. Placing his hand upon his breast he looks out of the page and speaks the beatings of his heart directly. Eadfrith tried his best to sustain that flow in his writing—by running some of the words together as speakers do, by leaving it to us readers to aspirate the unwritten vowels of *D(eu)m* and *D(eu)s* at the bottom of the page.

Yet as God's scribe even he could not stay entirely in the realm of the living. Many Oxen of the Aleph had to die to provide the vellum for him to write on. Some of the hairs still cling to it today. Probably his many coloured inks came from the sap of plants or from insects. Did he write with a dead bird's feather? We should never forget that about writing; it involves a death. In this case, however, the scribe redeems the butcher. *The hand that writes the Lord's Word acquires the ability to heal and to bless.*

Some 200 years later another writer, Aldred, took the spaces that Eadfrith left between the lines as invitation to add his Anglo-Saxon version to the text. He too knew the power of words. Calling himself an *unworthy and most miserable priest,* he offered his glossing of St John for the good of his own soul. Some of the old Rune magic still clings to his alphabet.

But Johnny Eagle never agitated his quill the way he did with Eadfrith, I fancy. Ignoring the lovely elisions of the script, Aldred divides word from word, vowel from colour, taking the inevitable step towards a more informational language.

Since then, of course, we have taken this crucifixion of the Word much further. How could language make us giddy now that every word comes processed through our fingertips? *In the beginning was the Word?* It was a Big Bang, surely; utterly loud and loveless.

 But who is this fair-haired person that stands beside the second 'I' of *principio?* It is (apart from the portraits of the four Evangelists) the only human figure to appear in this whole rendering of the Lindisfarne Gospels. Wide-eyed, gazing beyond the right-hand margin of the manuscript—it could be Eadfrith himself. If he could see me now—all my dictionaries and spellchecks—checking his spells and banishing my bewilderments.

It is a death, all right. So he wouldn't understand me if I said that some part of me is glad of it. It is good to sit here in my own sunlit room and not to have the Great Word of the Cosmos sounding through me. Let it rest for a while. Having typed my words I am free to look at them as marks on white paper. It is only through a language looked at that I become conscious of myself as thinker.

If it is Eadfrith there, leaning against that 'I' with the corners of his mouth downturned, then maybe he did have an inkling that in my day it would come to this. All the hieroglyphs and Godspells come to an end in us. We are free. To begin again. He was still inside the Beginning, held within its grace. Now, for good or ill, the Beginning is inside us and we must speak it.

Christ as Alphabet

Him? That's only God,
stepped down from the stars
to taste our vinegars.

That Fool—he scribbled
the one Word he was
into the wordless dirt.
He forgave his enemies!

Omega-and-Alph,
he hung there all afternoon
forsaken by himself.

He was the Word made flesh.
Five vowels   howled
through his open skin.
Three alphabets
were crucified with him.

The letter killeth, he said.

Hebrew, Latin and Greek,
binding in their intricate patterns
matters the stars once spoke.

Forgive me, dear Fool, if
with this pen I grave
you in the ground again.

It's only through such a death
that you can rise in our human breath.

Playing Judas

Somebody had to be Judas.
I chose this —
To play the Scorpion's part
And betray the Word with a kiss.

When the soldiers invaded the garden
He said, 'Friends, whom do you seek?'
I could have picked him out with a finger
But chose to kiss him on the cheek.

Twenty centuries of cursing
That kiss called down on my head.
He said to me, 'Go, do it quickly',
But first we dipped hands in the bread.

John, his beloved disciple,
Leaned in to the heart of his grace.
Only my part gave direction
To taste the salt on his face.

Bemused

The Girl Who Swallowed a Piano

I have swallowed a grand-piano. It doesn't show up on the x-rays, so it must be a glass one. I know it's there because sometimes late at night it wakes me with the sound of fingernails clicking across the keyboard.

How did it get there? Maybe it slipped in between mouthfuls of bread, or was it dissolved already in my mother's milk and then gathered inside me?

I rather liked it as a child—the faint strain of it along my arteries, or how the strings trembled whenever a car went past.

But some time before my fourteenth birthday such a music started up that night after night I kept the household awake with my dancing.

My mother said don't be silly. Just measure and see. No piano could fit there inside you. The doctor said what kind of music? Tell me who's playing it.

Nobody's playing it. It plays by itself—tunes I half recognize, but then faster and faster and so discordant that my guts get twisted around the strings.

Then suddenly the lid bangs shut and all the glass keys jangle together.

When you have a baby it will all settle down, they say. But I say there could never be room in there for both piano and baby. It would bump its head on the pedals. What if the lid slammed down on its pretty fingers?

Facing the Music

When I was fourteen I broke my leg playing Rugby. It must have been the Muse that tripped me. Unable to dance at the parties that Christmas I sat aside watching, suddenly awake to my separate presence in the Universe. And when the girls came to scribble their names on my plaster their eyes cast a glamour upon the light and changed it.

I returned to my boarding school. It was difficult being boys only. Girls were what we joked about, boasted about. Or else they were Goddesses . . . nothing in between. When the neighbouring girls' school joined us in the choir we gawped at them across an unbridgeable gulf. That was the pain of it; but perhaps it made some other song possible.

I began to read Wordsworth. When the other boys slipped into the night with their cigarettes I went to commune with Nature. It sounds priggish as I write it . . . would have done better to run with the others . . . except that She was waiting—The Woman-That-I'm-To-Marry. The trees there were too blatant. The stars were. I wanted to strip away the veil and find her.

I started to write poetry. *The shivering moon hangs silent o'er the trees*, was the first line I ever wrote. I blush now at the rhetoric, but at the time it thrilled me. Lying in bed that night I muttered it over and over—knew at last what I was born for.

A singing moon:

> *Come Goddess, to me alone you sing your song*
> *For these poor fools prefer to slumber on.*

The priggishness is there also; or does adolescence have authority to say such things, and now I have lost it?

So there she was, the Muse unashamedly, attendant at my initiation into poetry. And, looking through my present embarrassment, I admit that something which announced itself then carries forward in my work—the sense of a music at the heart of nature to be addressed and listened to.

Later I was to address her through the names of other women, imposing on them expectations they never could live up to. The tension between Muse and human continues to trouble me, yet gradually she has taught me not to be disdainful of household things—floors to be swept, chairs to be sat on. These too can borrow a curve of her.

She broods there all the time . . . on the underside. Some subtlety in the way the light falls and I am taken in.

Once in special the reds and greens of the neon flooding the Brighton streets suddenly declared her to me. She is the fire inside things, closer up and wilder than that cold moon lover who first sang to me.

This one is dangerous. She laughs at me from the rosebush. She comes to me now under a name which frightens me—Bella Donna, whose eyes grow wide with the juice of the Nightshade:

> *Beautiful Lady of Death, I'm numbered*
> *among the fools you croon to.*

Moon Caprice

I know a woman called Moon Caprice.
When she laughs she laughs in full.
When she cries she is the dark abyss.

That's what I love about her—
she does what she is.
When she folds away laundry
she forgets she ever had me for her lover.

Ah, but when she's with me
she takes oil from her cupboard
and as if I were the only one ever
she lards me all over.

Is she soul? Or is she sense?
Clothed only in that long nakedness of hers
she cancels out the difference.

Museum Piece

I'd give all
these haloed saints
for this one *Woman
Peeling a Parsnip*.

A dozen of my
crucifixions, too,
for the girl who
with such serenity
watches the white
skins curling
to the kitchen table.

The only thing
else I'd ask
is a frame in which
time could pause
for this benevolence
of light to hold me.

The Ground of Artemis

Last September we went to Ephesus to visit the ruined temple of Artemis. My wife's study of such things had prepared her for it. As for me, I wanted honey on my lips. In this temple dedicated to the Word I would ask a blessing for my work in poetry.

It was a Turkish woman with a wrinkled face who eventually swung the gate open. She tried to sell us a map of the site, but we already had one. My wife walked on ahead into the temple grounds. I lingered with the woman as she held out pretty rings and trinkets, coins, dug up from the strata of her ancient petticoats. I could see my wife beckoning from the ruins, but one of the coins had the bee of Ephesus stamped on it. This, surely, was authentic.

I handed the woman a note for I don't know how many thousand Lira, and immediately she bent down and wiped it in the dirt, brushed it across her lips, and at last I was free to enter.

My wife, however, intent on us exploring the Mysteries together, had grown annoyed at my loitering, and by the time I caught up with her she was quite unwilling to speak to me.

I liked the bee on that coin. I kept fingering it as I wandered alone among the chunks of marble. Here it is in front of me. I can scrape the oxides off with my thumbnail. This is not counterfeit.

—

Maybe the spirit of that place did loosen the language in me, because a few days later I wrote:

Only one column remains
to your temple, Artemis,
and how glad I am   to share
its narrow shade this morning
 with two girls two cows
and a fig tree as your peahens
squabble in the sun.

Yes, but it was sweetness I wanted, milk and honey—not that angry buzzing in my ear, not that wrinkled creature diddling me out of banknotes.

Who's to say, though, that to be stung in such a place isn't the more authentic? If I were to go there again I would thank the woman for that exchange of currency. And to my wife I say,

I am ready to go down now
not knowing fact from fiction
into the ground of Artemis.

Face to Face

In 1993, mid-December, shortly after my forty-ninth birthday, I found myself with friends in the foothills of the Sierra Nevada in California at an edge where the Yuba River tumbles out of the mountain.

That was a time when I had given up the place and position of work I had wound myself into for twenty-one years, and no news was yet reaching me from the future. It had left me vulnerable, I suppose, wide open to anything that might come to me in the moment.

Already, earlier that day, I had been drawn out of my usual self by a small gold leaf spinning in a spider's web. As I watched it in the morning sunlight it seemed to be an eye through which somebody was watching me. I was glad to be noticed.

But later, sitting on a rock beside that wild river, I felt that all those years of my work with teaching and poetry were like the scree on the mountainside. I was quietly grieving for that, and for what I saw at the time to be my inadequacy as a father.

Down below me I saw a rock carved by the water into the shape of a woman's hipbone, and all the while my companions handed me crackers with cheese and honey.

I looked at the grey cliff on the other side of the gully. Then I decided—I wouldn't look at the mountain. I wouldn't keep putting the world in its place with my busy eyesight. Thy will be done. I would let the mountain do the looking, and have its way with me.

Instantly a voice started up inside me—*Hallowed be thy Name,*
thy Name—all the pent kingdom of the place surging from the
rocky hollows. Forgiver-of-Trespass. Giver-of-Daily-Bread. Stern
and sheer He was, expecting something from us humans, though
infinitely patient.

Yes, I did have a work to do. But to keep my words true I would
have to take my future death into account—that was the contract.
Then He was gone. It was only the blind mountain. Crackers
and cheese. It was only the water pouring through that stony
hipbone.

What Sue Said

Is it true
what Sue said—
that a bee
in its lifetime
gathers one spoon-
ful of honey?

A Small Sweetness

As we drove into the mountains a strange feeling was rising inside me. I tried to ignore it,

but when we reached the snowline it suddenly spilled up into my eyes, and I said who needs philosophy or any books when this pure whiteness can give us everything?

You turned your eyes from the road a moment and said don't you know that this country has the highest rate of suicide among young people?

It was evening when we reached the other side of the mountain.

We walked into town past a group of loud swearing teenagers and into a bar where you ordered a liqueur and allowed me one sip of it.

That's mostly what I remember. That small sweetness.

Paul Evans: His Signature

Trust you to die on a mountain, Paul. You never cared for ropes called *God* or *Politics* or even *Career* to hold you, but lived fully somehow, always on the edge of falling, and I loved you for it.

When we were students together in Brighton, wandering on the beach instead of studying, you would climb up the stone jetties without a thought while I stood at the bottom holding the Mars Bars.

And here I am still holding them while you have gone on climbing beyond words somewhere, and I'd like to say that although I lost contact with you over the last years you were my first poet friend.

The honesty and clarity of your words stay with me as a mountain air, reminding me that poetry is not a clever way to write about the world but a way of seeing.

With some people their deaths belong to them as their lives do, and certainly in the way you fell I read your signature.

Raising the Spirits

Dear Guatemala Dobbs, I don't play the Ouija board anymore, but when I was twenty I couldn't help being eager for a source beyond the ordinary.

I come in atoms if you have circle. That's how you announced yourself. And when you explained 'atoms' by spelling *p.e.a.c.e.s.,* your love of wordplay, and that crazy name of yours somehow helped me to trust you.

Here's a piece you may remember:

> *Flashing flamingos,*
> *Breathing birds,*
> *Queens, kingfishers*
> *Sing dark reeds—*

Your one and only poem, was it? I don't suppose calling you up from the dead does you a service, really, but thank you anyway for troubling the waters of my thoughtless alphabet.

Give of your gold, you said. *Live and write.* And in the *circle of truth, poetry and love* which has indeed encompassed my life, I have tried (as you told me) to w*alk in the shadow of death,* and not to fear it.

I think right now as I write to you my pen is testing the verges. It's difficult to 'sing in the dark' and keep my hand entirely steady.

So Rare a Character
(*for Ashley on his birthday*)

1

Have you heard about the man who when he turned fifty-six
reached into the ear of Abraham's three-humped camel?

2

The scroll that he found there was writ in so rare a character
that even the nine Muftis of Qom failed to decipher it.

3

We can only speculate.

4

Could be it told of a Teller who having rhapsodized long
on the Nightingales in Fatima's garden
discerned a song closer that made his lip quiver.

5

Or. That he turned a stone over and found
nothing but worms and light.

6

Have you heard what the chickpea whispered to Ishmael?
'If you don't want to be baked,
lead your caravan in under the palm trees of Damascus.'

7

There's a man there, I'm told, who can hold fifty-six
chickpeas in the palm of his hand. He feeds them all to the camel
who carries his indecipherable story.

In the Blink

This morning I posted a letter
to the Grand Duchy of Luxemburg.
The postmaster said that's a grand
name for a place where if you blink
  you miss it.

Small things can be grand, of course.
A friend in the whole-food store
later confirmed this for me by saying
that her favourite programme
was of people sitting around in an abbey
  being silent.

You can miss many a grand thing
by blinking at the wrong moment.
That's probably why I have never seen
  a kingfisher.

As for the Second Coming
if you happen to blink at the split
second of its arrival you might never
suspect that the world had changed
during your brief absence from it.

Brief Encounter

I was sitting in my armchair wondering
why the Muse hadn't visited me lately
when the phone rang and a husky voice
said guess who and I said who and she
said Vera and I said sorry wrong number
that's why I couldn't guess and she said
oh what number did I dial then
and when I told her it turned out
she'd pressed a three instead of a two
and that was the end of our brief encounter.

Dear Sir,

I have recently discovered an Angel lodged in my ear, and this (as you might imagine) has somewhat distracted me from my worldly business.

I have reason to believe that the one I am referring to has been secretly transferring savings from my account into some other currency.

You make no mention of these transactions in my monthly statements so I can only assume that while the paper value of my money remains the same the aforesaid Angel, gathering the chink and glint of its gold, the lovely ruffle of the banknotes, has generated such an interest that your worthy establishment must be encountering some difficulty in ignoring it.

Any advice you could give me on this matter would be much appreciated.

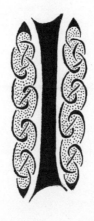

A More Dark Thing

Back to Babylon

This silver lyre lay in the Great
Death Pit five thousand years.

Somebody with a name made this,
embossed it with a bull's head, then
tenderly inlaid these eyes of Lapis.

Somebody's particular sadness
stroked these eleven strings.
Five thousand years under earth
could not still their murmurings.

Ælfred's Æstel

Ælfred had me wrought
  is how this Saxon gem
  (long dimmed
  under dirt) brags
  now in the daylight.

⁓

Was it a king then,
  deft with both sword
  and quill, first held
  its enamelled haft
  as he turned pages?

⁓

Ælfred brought scholars in,
  books in Latin, then
  with this wand's help
  made English what his
  quick eyes followed.

Our scholars fail to tell
why its lone figure
crafted in rich hues
holds flowers
or what his name is.

⁓

Weird worked it
that this broken trinket
fetched up from the fens
of Athelney should be so
rife with riddles.

⁓

This eyebright thing,
witness to its own making,
thrums in my ear: *Yes,
this is Ælfred Elf-Wise
in his counselling.*

⁓

*Giver-of-Gold. Word-
Friend.* What rune
might be rendered to me
as I dig among
your bones, Ælfred?

⁓

He was a chosen king.
The Un-things
had to rip at his gut
before he could read
the script of his name rightly.

A Tremor of the Lute

1

Dear Countess Marie,
I write this from another city
in an alien century
remembering the pleasure we took
in how a lute string
disappears when strummed.

That was at Poitiers.

Here in Central Park, New York,
fifty-one years old I stand, mute
before the beauty of a girl
not schooled in Courtliness.

Oh she was born learned.

Burn burn lust
into a lustre and let me tell
with what a grace she moves
as if some tremor of the lute
still sounded.

It was never winter in your songs.

Well, if you chanced this way
you would say a beauty's honed
by being momentary.

2

Knowing you once said
that *nobody can love*
unless they are compelled
by the eloquence of love
how is it that sometimes
in thought of you
all the words I blazoned
on my youth-time cloak
grow threadbare
and I fear to use them
falling to so deep a silence
that I must beg you of your grace
to grant this too
might be a form of eloquence.

3

What do I know of Courtesy
except that the Troubadour
leaves a gate open for Amor
to step lightly in, then
so demurely do his fingers
brush the strings that he
and his Lady to the Kingdom come
and find heart's ease
where lust and true devocioun
   speak the same.

A Gratitude
(*for Elizabeth Edmunds*)

Sit down, Elizabeth. This plastic chair
outside the Bridgeway Café in Sausalito
is empty especially for you,
and I have an hour to spare
before I catch the ferry.

You died four days ago five thousand
miles from where I sit in the sun
expecting any moment
a rumbling under San Francisco Bay
to shake the froth on my cappuccino.

It is a chair unfit, I confess,
to honour your ancient blood;
but before the currents carry you out
beyond the Golden Gate
I have a gratitude that must be spoken

for myself and anyone
who met you in the halls back home,
your sly smile, your gaze wide as ocean:
Thank you for speaking to the person
I could become.

Planta Genista

The Black Prince is in his tomb;
I saw that at Canterbury.
I thrive on this hillside
Beside the flowering broom
But want his chivalry.

Broom was the flower they loved,
Those high Plantagenets.
A sprig of the thing
Plucked by the wayside
Graced their coronets.

Eight kings borrowed a name
From that golden blazing.
Planta Genista upon the hill
Has filled my heart
With love-longing.

I had a crown once. Not gold
But a daisy chain.
The Flower of Princes
Sprawls in his cold grave.
He will not come again.

More than any earthly woman
War was his lover.
His black armour, hung
On the cathedral wall,
Is blazoned with bright flowers.

Clown Prince

As I sat by the road
the unmowed verges
tossed in a song from
before I was born
calling *Prince come home.*

I bent my ear to the stones
harkening furlongs back
to the trip
trap of the echo
of the shadow
of the horse of
whoever my father was.

It was a wind
of providence blustered
in the grass that morning.
Sprawled there in the dust,
I smiled
into every scorn-filled face:
I want to be a horseman
like my father.

Bare Names

My father is buried
in the churchyard here.
His gravestone makes
no mention of his fame
for (as the Vicar said)
it's only our bare names
we need when we are dead.

It's only our bare names
we own under the empty sky.
His absence is a presence.
His great granddaughter
who lacks all letters
brushes an ant from the stone
under which he lies.

This Tin Box

once fell on my father's head.
It was his only war wound.
All through my childhood
he used it to keep knick-knacks in,
and now I have it.

—

Many times
between Arromanches and West Berlin
he must've opened this black lid
to save a limb, a life,
or even to end one.

—

His name's not on it.
Nothing to say that this thing
clattered in a truck along rutted tracks,
the world on fire as I lay cradled.
He never told those stories.

The Living Room

The picture under which my father died
hangs over my fireplace now.

I always wanted it. This eagle on a pine bough
gazing upwards into the round ripe sun.

Always I assumed it was an evening coming on.
But now as I sit here in my own house

I think by his dying he has stitched a subtlety
between the eagle's eye and this red world that's rising,

and I am back with him two summers,
moving his deathbed into the living room.

That is what he wanted—to see how roses
burn in a window within the last word of a looking.

I was reading the resurrection to him when he stared
wildly into the sunlight and was gone.

Forgive Me This Trespass

I could use short words and still
not be able to reach her.

The first sign of it was
when she dialled her own number
and found it always engaged.

Now I visit her in a new place
where the nurse is kind,
and the bird she painted years ago
hangs on the wall, and her eyes
say I know that I know you.

Yes, it's Paul, your son. Then I lift
the spoon to her mouth and I sing to her,
tunes she crooned to me when I was young.

Last time she dialled a more dark thing
and all the pictures of her life started up —
her childhood in Hong Kong? Picnics
with her sisters beside the river?

Or the time she saw the Devil hovering
over her mirror and how Mrs Pogson said
only special souls are allowed that privilege.

I say the Lord's Prayer with her before I leave
and sometimes just for a moment
a wind of who she was passes over her face.

A Pocketful of Lies

I have a pocket.

I keep things in my pocket.

Buttons. Pieces of string. The iceberg
which sunk the *Titanic*.

Luckily it's a big pocket.

Thin, though. The melting ice
drips down my trouser leg.
The hammer they used at the crucifixion
keeps bumping my thigh as I walk.

Somebody has to look after things like that;

this silver spoon, I mean,
which so many Christmases
reflected my mother's face.

That's just the right pocket. The left one
is for the noises:

The nails hammered in. The whisper
of Rembrandt's paintbrush across his canvas.

And what about the sound the coat hangers made
as you shut the front door behind you?

Don't brush too close to my sides, or the cries
of the newly born will get mixed with the dying.

Excavating an Earlier Text

Forty years ago I wrote a poem about digging up *fragments of stained glass* in my garden. That was at Kings Langley when the medieval abbey and palace were being excavated.

Most of the glass crumbled when I touched it,
but here's a blue piece that I found . . . *a window
into the welkin where those old Dominicans
buried the secret of this colour.*

My use of the archaic word *welkin* instead of *sky* doesn't ring true now, but I do like the lines about holding that blue to the light to see *the Gothic letters dancing* inside it.

Today I showed it to my little grandson . . . a glimpse, forty winters gone, of his mother *born* as *a rainstorm shakes the window.*

I like the ring of the vowels at the end of the poem . . . *even the wind labours, tossing the dark pines. Richard II lay buried here for a time . . . a flurry of leaves and kings.*

Runes of Rain

Rain at Midnight

All right, I can hear you. What is it
you have come to tell me, Rain?

All the people I love are not here,
but maybe you have come in answer
   to my longing for them.

I suppose you have come to tell me
there's no end to longing, and I say
what about death—isn't that
   the end of it?

There never was a time, Rain, when I
did not love you. You are oil and balm.
So, tell me what it's for—this no end
   of longing.

What if I stopped thinking there could
be an end to it and simply lived it?

I could die, I think, out beyond longing,
into the small sounds of you on the roof
   and be only the listening.

Twelve Windows

Here we are
in a room
with twelve windows.

As we listen
we are looked at
by the twelve disciples
by the twelve
signs of the Zodiac.

This is a lie
but I believe it.

Please believe it too
or the room
shrinks to a size
that won't contain us.

The Night I Heard Something Knocking at My Window

Is it you, little snail? —
dragging your spiral house
across the stars.

It makes me smile
that such a lowly one
should live so earnestly

and that a sound so intimate
could quite drown out
the empty roar of night.

Longing for Morning

It was after midnight. I was afraid
my taxi in the drive would wake you.
Your note in the caravan
gladdened my heart
after all that distance between us.

~

It was cold in there.
And then a big wind arose
and shook the sides of the van
and rattled down walnuts on the roof
as I lay there longing for morning.

~

I slept, I suppose, then woke
dishevelled and unshaven,
wondering whether you'd like me
with my hair turning grey.

~

A statue of the Three Graces
showed the pathway to your door,
but I glanced in through a window
and there you were, spooning porridge
into the mouth of your baby.

Winter Plainsong

No clothes are jiving
on the white line strung
from the bare birch tree

but it twangs suddenly
as the sparrow fails
to take a foothold.

The smallest wind
can shake it—sigh
of somebody I love
yet rarely think of;

or the cathedral, five
time zones away,
collapsing on its worshippers.

'Impossible to imagine'
is the official word for it,
yet everything tries to.

The unused clothes pegs
notate a plainsong
that insists on winter.

As If

This window
where nettles
shake. These
runes of rain
fretting the ivy.
I could keep
telling. This.
And then this.
While someone
in the distance
hammers on stone.
Keep naming
as if to snare
in my book
one moment.
Make it history.
That a nettle
shook. That ivy
trembled
in November rain.
I'm writing it down.
As if to test
is this any less
momentous than
towers falling
in a far off town.

What If

The dormitory at school I remember
my thin grey blanket
the noise on the radio
that Alfred Hinds had escaped from jail
and that once again
he was prowling in the dark of Dartmoor
the bloodhounds
sniffing among the bogs and crags
and what if
he came down to the town where I was
into the smells and corridors
where I so far from home was
holding my breath
for the clang of his heels
on the iron fire escape
yet secretly I admired him
faceless one with the thin name
who could shimmy out through the bars
and on to the moor
to be one with the wind
whining in the gorse not anyone
able to bind him

Wishing To Be Lorenzo

There was rain on the path last night.
I was walking home from a play
which pitted blood against convention:

It is not my fault, Lorenzo said.
It is the fault of perfume
wafting out of dark ringlets.

I was murmuring that to myself,
kind of wishing I'd said it,
as the path dipped down

into this fault of earth
where I have lived year on year.
I could see the lights in my window.

I will stand on the hill, sighed Lorenzo,
and let the rain play in my hair.

Everything Speaks

I went down to the end of the lane,
crossed the small stream,
and started to climb the hill
behind our house.

Usually I enjoy that walk
but today it seemed dank and paltry.

When I reached the edge of the Forest
I glanced back into the valley
to see how small my life was.

A white plastic bag was hanging
from a branch above my head.
The logo on its side said,
We are open whenever you need us.

Into the Numberless

This time of day the Forest
gathers the measured greens
back into the numberless.

This writhing mass. It seems
to be the thought of something
and it knows I think so.

Keep to the bridle paths
its daytime signs instruct.

But, as the birdsong swells
then slowly fades, it grows
too dark to read by.

Already beyond the glades
the thud from the gunnery
is starting up. The Forest hums.

Relinquish what you love.
There is no map for this.

Bird of Morning

1

Rainy evening.
Car splashes by.

You can't hear it.
Your ear

tuned to the first
bird of morning.

But, turn a little
this way, Angel.

It's only the thickness
of the earth between.

2

I'm watching the pulse in my thumb
as it comes and goes in the light
this Wednesday morning.

It is mine, I suppose;
yet it throbs to a will so dark
I cannot really claim it.

I suppose it could stop.
Then I'd have no further need
for Wednesdays or mornings,

and this young blackbird
cocking its head at me
from the top of the molehill

would slip to oblivion. Sing, sing
little soul. There's a secret pulse
from the ring finger into the heart.

3

If the doctor
tossed me up in the air
it was to test his theory
that even the newly born
are afraid of falling.

I could have complained,
but wonder instead
what not yet
known about bird I was
clutching out for.

The doctor's gone. I'm glad
to be alive, shaping
and releasing this little fist-
ful of song which
caught me as I was falling.

4

As I walked out this May morning
I heard the Blackbird
calling from the wood

and there without a word
the Bluebells spread and I said
look at me you pure inquisitors

and this they did—
their mute gaze finding out a joy
I'd too long shaded from the view

and as the Blackbird
carolled in the sunlit glade
I wept for being seen through.

Loosening the Brickwork

With Pen in Mind

When using a pen
to write about one surely
the model is at hand.

Wrist moves it. Mind
reads there and says oh
I am a signifier.

Mark how the mind
served by the hand stirs
what is mentioning itself.

It shapes the word 'pen'
which is only a stain
upon white unless the mind
quickens the sense of it.

This thin nib commits
meaning to matter.
It patterns the whiteness.

What Poetry Serves

It serves community. It serves the quality of our relationships. When I stand in the presence of somebody I love the fullest destiny of my words is poetry.

Today, writing this, it is language I stand in the presence of. It, too, needs to be loved. A language that is merely used will soon turn desolate.

Poetry is one way of loving language. It gives words a context whereby lost roots are stirred, new meanings potentized.

It reminds me that *com-pan-ions* were once bread-fellows, and that a Grace well spoken makes fellow communicants of those who share my table.

Such a loving and laving of words works homeopathically. Though only a few may read it, a word quickened within a poem filters down till it is found even in the mouths of those who despise poetry.

言
霊

> The Japanese call this *Kotodama* —
> the Spirit of a Word. That Spirit
> needs to be cared for. Otherwise,
> it abandons its earthly vehicle.

A graceless word is not a neutral thing. Husks of meaning work destructively — not bread enough to serve communion with.

In the act of writing poetry we stand at a verge of consciousness. Past language momentarily comes to an end and then, as dew on the wheat, is given back to us. As frost on a knifeblade. Is given back to us.

And the act of reading a poem? It serves perception. One way of keeping shine on a stone is to leave it where you find it. Another is to hold it in the wash of poetry.

My Japanese friends told me another thing—that the larynx is shaped like the Buddha, and that *Buddha-Throat* is actually their name for it.

How happy and terrified I am to learn that my every utterance passes through Buddha's place. There he sits—close as I am to myself—witness to what truth or beauty rings in the words I speak.

It was *Right Speech* he advocated in his Eightfold Path—a love-filled language and a language loved. Poetry is the practice of it.

Dear Mr Blake,

Do you have a dictionary in your present household? And does it, like mine, define a sentence as a 'grammatically correct expression of a complete thought'? I wonder what you think of that. Such grammar makes upright citizens but fails to satisfy. I want to juxtapose it with your dictum: 'Poetry Fetter'd Fetters the Human Race'. What is a 'complete thought' anyway? Grammar is no set of correctnesses imposed on words; it is a breath which rolls through them. Your *Tyger* burns the brighter for not being spelt correctly.

Once I was invited to speak to a group of twelve-year-olds. At the end of a long day I asked what I should talk about. One girl, already feeling the weight of those 'fetters', stood up and said, 'Teach us the connection between language and the soul.' I can't remember how I responded, but it struck me later that my whole work has been devoted to the answering of her marvellous question.

My dictionary goes on to tell me that 'sentence' derives from the Latin 'sententia' (an opinion); but I'm tracing it deeper to 'sentire', to sense, to feel into the life of things. Every e-motion in the heart seeks its equivalent within the com-motion of the words we speak.

As for my grammar book, it lists four kinds of sentence —Statement, Question, Exclamation and Command. Whatever we say or write is sentenced to be one of them. It only fetters us however if we abstract the fact of it from the rest of the cosmos. I'd tell the girl if I could that language is a cosmos among others, that its dynamics are revealed in the elements of Earth, Water, Air and Fire which you, Sir, knew to be creative powers behind the veil of nature. A grammar book is a map of the soul if we read it right, and when these four hallows of language arise as showings of our deepest temperament we acknowledge them to be Scripture.

You are a master of statement. Your own vision, together with your deep reading of the Bible, leads you beyond the clarity and 'correct expression' that we demand of statement, to some authentic inner source of knowing. I hear it in your Proverbs: 'The Tygers of Wrath are wiser than the Horses of Instruction'. How you raged against those instructors who, through their rational statements inspired by 'the Daughters of Memory', poured scorn on 'the Daughters of Inspiration' that you served. 'The tree which moves some to tears of joy is in the eyes of others only a green thing that stands in the way', is your response to one of them. I can't deny that the ability to stand back from the world, to see a 'thing' and make free and clear pronouncements about it, was perfected by 'Bacon, Locke and Newton', the very ones who stirred the wrath in you. Having said that, though, if we stay content with this defining faculty then syntax becomes an axe to cut the 'green thing' down and we see no reason to shed any tears about it.

You are also a brave questioner. As you cast your words into the fire of *Tyger*, questioning beomes a quest—'Did He who made the Lamb make thee?'—to meet the essence of an Other. You learnt that from your beloved 'Book of Job', I'm sure, where in a whirlwind of questions God annihilates Job's pride until all he can say is, 'Behold I am vile; what shall I answer thee?' The power of interrogation, most deeply exercised, allows Job to break through the veil and meet the fiery Leviathan (model, surely, for your *Tyger*'s 'fearful symmetry'). Yet you are painfully aware of the shadow side of the act—'the idiot Questioner . . . who publishes doubt and calls it knowledge'. It is not easy to purge our words in the fire and be a conduit for these founts of language.

I do not doubt that out of heart's abundance you were a great exclaimer of life—'O Rose', 'Ah, Sunflower'— lifting praise and lamentation (as the psalmist does) to the point where 'exuberance is beauty', and everything we behold is 'holy'. I can well understand, however, that 'aspersions of madness' might be cast on those who dare to stand at such an edge of language.

It was not my intention to praise you overmuch, but 'there are some that have the power of sentences' (said Christopher Smart) and you are one of them. Why else would your written characters break free sometimes into snakelike twists and pictures? Even when they do submit to referential restraints this commanding power declares itself in the way your poetry contains some of the strongest imperatives in the language. 'Hear the voice of the Bard' (that's one of them) — encouraging each of us to attend to the 'Holy Word' that the girl I spoke of must have been sensing. Then in the same poem you call with supreme confidence and good will — 'O Earth, O Earth return!' — rousing the planet herself to cast off the fetters of dead letters which bind our perception of her.

The poetry of your time abounds with elemental energy — Shelley, invoking the West Wind to storm through his words; you, daring to seize the fire. Most famously there is Coleridge with his garden of dancing rocks, and the sacred river Alph bursting out of the ground. What's that but the torrent of living language breaking free from the 'mind-forged' restrictions that the Royal Society of Science was attempting to cast upon it? It meandered above ground during the lives of your great contemporaries; but already the river Thames was being 'chartered' within its stony embankments, and the insistence on sentence as 'grammatically correct expression' could not be resisted. Sentenced thus by sentences, we make our brain paths visible in the way we walk and, soon enough, our walking writes its grids and structures and 'improvements' into the living landscape. You are right, Mr Blake, 'Poetry Fetter'd Fetters the Human Race'. A girl asked me a question; you are the fire to test my words by as I seek to answer it.

Slippery Characters

What John Keats proclaims from his gravestone—that his name is *writ in water*—is a fine motto to live and write by. It is my constant theme, in fact—this longing to loosen the brickwork of the written character. In reading back, though, I am startled to find that the same ungraspable spirit informs so many of the human characters who inhabit these pages:

Pages 11 & 80. *Christopher Smart*: I am quoting from what remains of his 'Jubilate Agno', written one line a day in a lunatic asylum. Another fragment, *For in my nature I quested for beauty, but God, God hath sent me to sea for pearls,* shows he had worked a few bricks loose already.

Pages 11 & 12. Similarly, *Arthur Rimbaud* (in 'The Drunken Boat') finds himself *bathing in the poem of the sea* . . . set adrift by hashish rather than God, perhaps. (See Bernard's Penguin translation.)

Page 12. *Robert Duncan* visited Cambridge, Brighton, and London in the late 1960s/early 70s. Contact with him and his work at that time, and later in San Francisco, inspired my attempt in this book to explore personal biography at the verge of the mythological. The lines quoted are from his poem, 'The Natural Doctrine'.

Page 14. *Humbaba*: The Sumerian *Epic of Gilgamesh* (buried for two thousand years) tells how this 'monstrous' guardian of the forest is killed by Gilgamesh whose destiny it was to have his own name *stamped on brick*. I have enhanced the more feminine aspects of Humbaba's character.

Page 17. In an early poem about Lindisfarne I had the North Sea *rolling like the wrinkled scriptures.*

Page 21. *Christ* as clown, or holy fool: In St John's apocryphal gospel Christ says of himself: *In a word, I am the Word who did play all things*. I have taken this as permission for entertaining Him in these pages outside the binding of conventional theologies.

Page 22.   *Judas*: thief and betrayer, he may be; yet many have speculated as to whether his part in the Easter drama was more heroic and sacrificial than the official text allows for.

Page 25.   *The girl who swallowed a piano*: that's Princess Alexandra of Bavaria, 1826-75, who suffered this delusion though in later life, and in a time before x-rays and cars were invented.

Page 30.   *Artemis*: Her temple at Ephesus was one of the wonders of the ancient world. The doctrine of the creative Word emerged there through Heraclitus and Cratilus, culminating in the gospel which John wrote in that city.

Page 35.   *Paul Evans*: In the late 1960s we sat around in the Brighton pubs, plotting to undermine the establishment through our poetry magazine, 'Eleventh Finger'. I drank orange juice. He died in 1991, climbing Snowdon.

Page 36.   *Guatemala Dobbs*: an utterly elusive character.

Page 44.   *The Ælfred Jewel* in the Ashmolean Museum in Oxford is one of the magic treasures of Britain. Though the scholars 'fail to tell', they helpfully suggest that the figure depicted on Ælfred's ceremonial 'æstel' (or bookmarker) could be Eyesight itself standing among flowers.

Page 46.   *Marie of Champagne* (daughter of Queen Eleanor of Aquitaine) was a main inspirer of the Troubadour poetry. Some say it was she who decided that the marriage ring has its rightful place on this most 'sinister' of fingers. The quotation, recorded by Andreas Capelanus, is a judgement from the 'Courts of Love' presided over by the Countess.

Page 49. *The Black Prince*: Prince Edward was the oldest son of King Edward III, dying before he could come to the throne. Richard II was his son.

Page 50. *The Clown Prince* must be 'the child of Europe', Kaspar Hauser. He is the pure uneducated soul who in 1828 appeared out of nowhere on the streets of Nuremberg. Some claim that he was indeed a prince, rightful heir to the House of Baden.

Page 56. *Richard II*: In Shakespeare's play of that name a poignant scene takes place in the palace garden at Langley. Last of the Plantagenet kings, we see him in the 'Wilton Diptych' wearing a necklace of broom pods (planta genista).

Page 65. *Alfred Hinds*: Twentieth-century criminal who kept on escaping from his confinement. When the prison authorities took mug-shots of him he distorted his face so that nobody would recognize him when he was on the run.

Page 66. *Lorenzo* can be found in Lorca's 'Blood Wedding'.

Page 68. *The Forest hums*: The Ashdown Forest, in fact, where Winnie-the-Pooh (who couldn't read an A when he saw one) composed his 'Hums'.

Page 84. *Paul Matthews* taught for many years at Emerson College in the south of England. He has travelled with his work in USA, Australia, New Zealand, Germany, Norway, Sweden and in the UK. His explorations of the creative process are gathered in his books, *Sing Me the Creation* and *Words in Place* (Hawthorn Press). He was the founder of *Poetry OtherWise*. An earlier gathering of his poetry is *The Ground that Loves Seeks* (Five Seasons Press).

Names and Fames

Matthews was my father's name. His father was the Dean of St Paul's Cathedral, and because of that my mother (with me curled inside) sheltered in the crypt as the bombs were falling.

Paul: The very fame of the place, resounding in the brickwork, bound and rounded my skull, my tongue, into this echoing dome I'm sentenced to carry about with me.

And this *Michael* lurking between the names I'm known by? It is my uncle, killed at Dunkirk. When I was born at Michaelmas my brow was already wet with his unsung words and purposes.

As for *Forster*—it is the mixing into the proprieties of my London tongue of my mother's maiden sing-song out of Northumberland so that no one guesses where I come from.

Paul Michael Forster Matthews: two saints and an angel. Oh let me be the nobody I am, curled as a shell, attending to the things I speak, humming with what I listen.

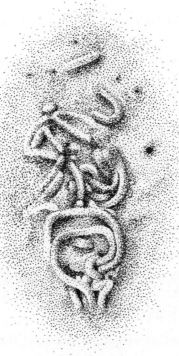

God be praised in the Lugworm
whose scriptures in the sand imbue
the illuminations of the holy scribes